Garboldisham is an attractive village, lying hidden away from the Thetford to Diss road, but the sign stands on this road at the road junction. At the top of the post with its finely carved motifs is a model of the post mill, a feature of the village, now restored to use.

EAST ANGLIAN
VILLAGE AND TOWN SIGNS

Ursula Bourne

Shire Publications Ltd

CONTENTS

British Library Cataloguing in Publication data available.

Printed in Great Britain by C. I. Thomas & Sons (Haverfordwest) Ltd, Press Buildings, Merlins Bridge, Haverfordwest Dyfed SA61 1XF.

COVER: **Redgrave** village is in Suffolk, a few miles west of Diss, and its carved and painted sign, erected in 1983, stands on the village green, known as the Knoll. On one side, with the fourteenth-century church, the old barn, now converted into cottages, and the windmill, destroyed by fire in 1924, the monks are a reminder that the Abbot of Bury was lord of the manor, and the organ commemorates the Hart family, local organ builders, who built an organ for Mendelssohn. The other side depicts Redgrave Fen — old peat cuttings — and the very rare raft spider which is to be found there. The boar surmounting the sign is the crest of the Bacon family; Sir Nicolas Bacon, Lord Keeper to Elizabeth I, built the old Redgrave Hall.

North Repps, a small village a few miles south of Cromer, possesses a very fine carved and painted sign which stands high in a prominent position at the meeting of several roads. On it are eleven items associated with the parish or with persons who have lived in it.

Flitcham. St Felix of Burgundy, who founded the Christian church in Norfolk, is said to have sailed up the Babingley river to start his evangelical mission in the village of Flitcham. He is seen on the sign, holding his crook, in the stern of a ship.

INTRODUCTION

Village signs, which should not be confused with inn signs, are a feature of the East Anglian countryside. They can be found in other parts of Britain, but the number in East Anglia far exceeds that anywhere else, Norfolk alone having over three hundred. This book includes a good selection of them.

Kind Edward VII had the original idea that, to encourage appreciation of and interest in their villages, the inhabitants should erect village signs, and this was continued by his son George V and grandson George VI. The first signs were erected in the villages on the Sandringham estate and were made in what is now known as the Queen's Carving School.

In 1929 the enterprise received an important stimulus from Harry Carter, a nephew of the renowned Egyptologist Howard Carter, excavator of Tutankhamun's tomb. Born in London and trained at the Slade College of Art, Harry Carter became the arts and technical crafts master of Hamonds Grammar School in the Norfolk town of Swaffham. He became interested in the village sign venture and in 1929 made his first sign, which was erected in Swaffham. Harry Carter afterwards made a great number of signs throughout East Anglia, and even further afield, before his death. His signs are so distinctive that they can be easily identified. They are all carved in wood and brightly painted. His work was meticulous in every detail. A great deal of thought and study went into each sign, which might take him between six months and a year to complete.

One of his problems was obtaining the right wood. It had to be properly seasoned, and though he believed English oak, because of its strength and durability, was the best, he had sometimes to use other woods, such as mahogany or walnut. After painting, the signs were varnished. Instead of gold paint he preferred to use gold leaf because, although it was more expensive, it stood up better to the weather.

Deterioration through exposure to the weather has always been a problem with signs and to keep them in perfect condition they need an occasional refurbishing. Unfortunately, a beautifully executed sign may be neglected, and the colours may become faded and dim. Various devices have been used to protect a sign. One is the provision of a small roof over it, as for example at Drinkstone. Another is to encase a painted sign in a frame with a sheet of glass over it; but unfortunately this does not always provide sufficient protection.

Carved and painted signs similar to Harry Carter's are to be found in many villages, often the work of local artists and craftsmen. There are also some beautiful, though less conspicuous, carved signs which are unpainted — one being the statue of a falconer in Earl Soham. Pictures on plain board, in the style of the usual inn sign, are fairly common, but the sign at Middleton, made in mosaic by a local artist, is probably unique.

A different type of sign, found particularly in Suffolk villages, is that made of wrought iron. These, often the work of a local blacksmith, may be either black or brightly coloured, and many are very striking, standing out sharply against the sky. A good example is the decorative and brightly painted one at Kenninghall. A highly original metal sign is that at Stibbard, constructed of farm implements and metal bits and pieces.

Signs are usually fixed on a post, and the base is often made of a local stone.

The occasion for the erection of a sign is often the commemoration of a centenary or of an event such as the Queen's Silver Jubilee in 1977, when a large number of signs were erected. Those responsible may be the village community as a whole, a private donor or, frequently, the local Women's Institute.

The subject of a sign may be a landmark of the village or town, a local product, craft or industry, a legend or an event in its history, or simply a play on the name.

The siting of signs varies. Where there is a village green or grassy triangle, the sign is often placed in a conspicuous position there. In other cases it may be in a commanding position at the entrance to the village. This may necessitate two signs, one at either end, unless, as at Walberswick, which is bounded on one side by the sea and on another by the river, there is only one main road by which the village can be entered.

Some people regard East Anglia as including not only Norfolk and Suffolk but also parts of Cambridgeshire and north Essex, but in this book only the counties of Norfolk and Suffolk are included.

The signs are most attractive features of their town or village and they could even form the basis for a holiday in the region, or for a day's outing. In this book they have therefore been arranged according to area, starting from the villages on the Sandringham estate in north-west Norfolk, where they originated.

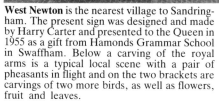

West Newton is the nearest village to Sandringham. The present sign was designed and made by Harry Carter and presented to the Queen in 1955 as a gift from Hamonds Grammar School in Swaffham. Below a carving of the royal arms is a typical local scene with a pair of pheasants in flight and on the two brackets are carvings of two more birds, as well as flowers, fruit and leaves.

Shernborne. The village sign was originally commissioned by King Edward VII when he was still Prince of Wales but has since undergone several alterations in detail. The two figures represent Sir Thomas Shernborne and his wife Jamona, to whom there are bronzes, dated 1438, in the church.

Anmer was once a Roman encampment on the Peddars Way and the figure of a Roman soldier is shown on one of the two sides of the sign. On the other is a boy scout, recording that the sign was the gift of the Boy Scouts of Norfolk to the Queen, in gratitude for her interest in the movement.

Babingley also has a sign (not illustrated) depicting St Felix. According to legend he was shipwrecked on his voyage to Britain and saved by a family of beavers; in return he made the father beaver a bishop. The sign shows St Felix with a ship in the background and, above, the beaver family, with the father in a red robe and mitre, holding a crook.

King's Lynn at one time had three signs: one near the river, but this is no longer there; another on the Gayton road leading into the town from north Norfolk; and a third, shown here, by the Hardwick road near the dual carriageway. This is two-sided. On one side appears St Margaret, to whom one of the town's churches is dedicated, and who is reputed to have slain a dragon with her spear; and on the other Henry Bell stands before the Lynn Custom House, of which he was the architect.

Watlington lies a few miles south of King's Lynn. The sign stands at a road junction in the village, opposite the Angel. It depicts the distribution of loaves of bread under an eighteenth-century charity by which twelve loaves of bread are given on alternative Sundays to poor widows of Watlington and the neighbouring village of Tottenhall.

Wolferton. The sign illustrates the Norse legend of the giant wolf Fenrir, who, to show his strength in breaking bonds, consented to be bound if the god Tyr would put his right hand in his mouth; but the bonds proved unbreakable and so Tyr lost his hand.

East Winch, a village a few miles south-east of King's Lynn, combined with its neighbour West Bilney to produce one of the loveliest of all village signs. It stands just off the main road beside the nature reserve of the Norfolk Naturalist Trust and shows the wildlife of the district, with the churches of the two villages in the background.

North Runcton is a village south-east of King's Lynn. Its early eighteenth-century church, built of the local carr-stone, is attributed to Henry Bell, who built the Custom House in King's Lynn. The sign stands at the corner of the green by the church. It shows the church with Henry Bell standing at one side, and below are the arms of the Gurney family, long associated with the village.

Heacham, a village a few miles south of Hunstanton, possesses a most attractive sign. This stands on the main road at the turning opposite the Norfolk Lavender fields. Princess Pocahontas, the daughter of a Red Indian chief, married a Heacham man, John Rolfe. She came to England and was presented at court; on the sign she is portrayed in the court dress of the period. She is supported by two horses, one a 'sea-horse' to mark Heacham's links with the sea, and the other recalling a hackney breed for which the village was famous. Below, with a starfish, is a bunch of lavender, symbolising the Norfolk Lavender products for which Heacham is now famous.

Snettisham is on the main road from King's Lynn to Hunstanton, and the sign is on the left side on entering, just before the hump-backed bridge. It is a striking sign, for it is surmounted by a golden torque, a representation of one found in a nearby field. This is supported by two sea-horses, and beside them are two smugglers and, in the distance, a square-rigged smugglers' craft, a reminder that smugglers once frequented this part of the coast.

Hunstanton, a seaside resort overlooking the Wash, is the only resort in East Anglia which faces west. Its sign, which stands on the large central green on the sea front, shows the sun setting over the sea. The figures are those of St Edmund and the wolf which, according to legend, guarded his head after he had been beheaded by the Danes. There is a cliff named St Edmund's Point, and local legend has it that St Edmund landed here on his way to be crowned king of East Anglia.

Brancaster, on the north Norfolk coast, is the *Branodunum* of Roman times, but today it is a holiday centre, with many new houses, and there are few remains of the Roman fort, which stood between the village and the Staithe. But the Staithe still maintains its connections with the sea, as the village sign shows, for here is the head of a Roman soldier flanked by sea-horses. The sign is on the main road from Wells to Hunstanton, almost opposite the church.

Swaffham. The two-sided sign stands on one side of the market place and was the first to be made by Harry Carter — in 1929. It shows the fifteenth-century pedlar John Chapman, with his dog and a crock of gold. According to the story, Chapman dreamt that if he went to London Bridge he would hear something to his advantage. He went, with his dog, and met a man who told him that he had dreamt that if he went to Swaffham and dug under an apple tree in the garden of a pedlar he would find a crock of gold. The pedlar hastened home and dug under his apple tree and found not one but two crocks of gold. Becoming a wealthy man, he gave money for the building of a new north aisle to the church.

Castle Acre lies a few miles north of Swaffham. The ruined priory is worthy of a visit, as is the village, built in the outer bailey of the ruined castle. The sign, standing in the village centre, shows a reconstruction of the original priory, built by William de Warenne, a follower of William the Conqueror, and, below, a monk of the Cluniac order, for which the priory was built.

Shouldham village, midway between Swaffham and Downham Market, was once a market town and the site of a priory. The sign, which stands on one side of the green, shows, against a background of the priory ruins, a monk and a drover with his animals on the way to market. The well on the shield below represents the Silver Well, a source of a natural mineral water near the village.

Marham, to the west of Swaffham, once had a Cistercian nunnery but is best known today for the Royal Air Force station situated in the parish. The sign, standing by the church, was given to the village on the occasion of the Queen's Silver Jubilee by the RAF to show their appreciation of its hospitality. A Cistercian nun stands in the centre and the side panels show the local pumping station, a plough representing agriculture, an aeroplane of earlier design symbolic of the role of RAF Marham in two world wars, and a bunch of cherries reminiscent of the time when the village was known as Cherry Marham because of the abundance and excellence of the cherries grown there.

Feltwell lies north-west of Brandon. The sign stands in the garden of the Oak Street Almshouses and is not easy to find. Alveva, a Saxon woman who once owned part of the village, stands in the centre of the sign and behind are two large trees, an oak with a girth of 32 feet 6 inches (9.9 m), said to have been thirteen hundred years old when felled in 1964, and an elm felled two years before. The sheep represent ancient sheep walks and the church is shown as it was before the tower fell while under repair in 1898.

Downham Market is notable for its many Norfolk carr-stone buildings. Its sign, which was erected in 1965 to mark the fiftieth anniversary of the founding of the Downham Market Women's Institute, is two-sided. On one side St Winnold is seen ringing a bell, which, according to legend, caused fish to rise, and on the other young Nelson is playing with a toy ship — a reminder of Nelson's attendance at the local grammar school. One of the two small spandrels on either side of these panels bears the WI emblem and the other a butter churn, butter making having once been a local industry. The two white horses surmounting this handsome sign are a reminder of the horse fairs once held in the town, and they support a shield bearing the arms of Edmund, the martyr king, to whom the church is dedicated. The sign is situated in the town on the London road.

Brandon, on the Norfolk-Suffolk border, has long been noted for flint knapping, a trade which is still carried on there. In olden times the flints were brought from the nearby mines known as Grimes Graves. The sign, standing near the road junction at the southern end of the town, shows flint knappers at work.

Wretham. The group of villages known as the Wrethams is situated around the A1025 road from Thetford. Surrounded by the forested countryside of Breckland, it is an area of wild beauty, and the fine sign of coloured aluminium, which is to be found on the main road at the entrance to the village, depicts this; the witch and her cat flying across on her broomstick symbolise the belief in witchcraft in these remote areas. The ram's head surmounting it recalls an annual custom of the past, when the authorities of Eton College, which owned East Wretham, released a ram in a field, to be taken by whomever could catch it.

Hockham Magna, north-east of Thetford, was known in the past for the annual Hockham Horn Fair, at which objects of all kinds made of horn were sold. This was also the occasion for the appearance of the Horned Man who, in a horned head-dress, 'attacked' and chased strangers until they gave him money. The carved and painted sign, which stands on the village green, records this occasion in medieval times.

Thompson, a remote village a few miles south of Watton, stands beside the Peddars Way, an ancient track which ran from Holme on the Norfolk coast of the Wash, and its carved oak sign, which stands on the green at the cross-roads, has figures of some who would have travelled that way. The coat of arms below is that of the Shardelow family, who founded a small college here in the fourteenth century.

Caston, a few miles south of Watton, had in medieval times a refectory which was visited by pilgrims on their way to the shrine at Walsingham. This later became Church Farm, and the gable end forms the background to the scene of pilgrims on the sign, which stands on the green before the church and in sight of Church Farm.

Watton has a gold-painted sign standing in the long High Street. Its theme is the story of the Babes in the Wood. It is reputed that the wood in the story is the nearby Wayland Wood, and that the wicked uncle lived in the neighbouring Griston Hall. The hare jumping over the tun represents the name Watton, 'wat' being a country word for a hare.

Saham Toney a village just north of Watton, has a fine church, by which the village sign stands, and nearby is a mere which is said to have appeared in a night. The mere, backed by numerous trees, is shown on the sign, and the boat with two clerical fishermen recalls that the monks from Castle Acre Priory were allowed to fish in the mere twice a year. The figure in the foreground, with his dog, is Sir Roger Toni, an early lord of the manor.

Brisley lies on the road from East Dereham to Fakenham, and the carved and coloured sign is by this road beside the church. Against a background of the church is the figure of Richard Taverner, who was born in the village and died in 1573. A scholar of both Oxford and Cambridge, he wrote and published an English translation of the Bible.

East Dereham. This busy town has an unusual sign which bridges the High Street. It was given by the Rotary Club in 1954 to mark the town's existence since 654. St Withburg, one of the saintly daughters of the Saxon king Anna, was first buried in East Dereham, though later her remains were removed by the monks to Ely. The sign, illustrating a legend, shows two does being pursued by a huntsman and seeking protection from the saint.

Ashill, south-east of Swaffham, has an attractive sign beside the large village green. The geese on the sign recall that, under the Enclosure Acts of the eighteenth century, each family in the village was allowed to graze not more than four geese on the green.

Stibbard, a village a few miles east of Fakenham, possesses a unique and arresting sign. It is the work of an internationally renowned sculptress, Ros Newman, and represents the agricultural life of the village for it depicts a ploughman at work. He and his plough are made from all manner of farm implements and bits and pieces of metal. The sign, which stands near the school, warrants time to study, for it is a fascinating work of art.

Gunthorpe, a rural village possessing a number of flint houses, lies between Fakenham and Holt. The sign, which stands on a grass triangle in the village at the junction of several roads, depicts two village benefactors who left legacies for the poor in what is known as the Malthouse Pightle Charity, the money being obtained from the rent of a small field or 'pightle'.

Fakenham has a two-sided sign which because of its siting is not seen to the best advantage. It stands at Leaches Corner, opposite the post office. The man at a printing press on the panel on one side represents the town's main industry. On the panel on the other side is the figure of Samuel Peckover, a Quaker and Cromwellian who opened Fakenham's first bank. The symbols on the brackets commemorate four other famous Fakenham men.

Thursford lies on the Fakenham to Holt road and its sign stands on a triangle of grass at Thursford Green. Nearby is the Thursford Collection of steam engines and mechanical organs and reference to this appears on the sign, along with many other items, which are described on a panel below the sign.

Great Walsingham won an award as the best kept village in 1972 and to commemorate this the inhabitants erected the sign, which stands on a small green in the centre of the village. The squirrel partly encircled by oak leaves is the crest of the Lee Warner family, long connected with the village.

Wells-next-the-Sea is a small town on the north Norfolk coast and its sign stands on the main road at the Holkham end. It was given by the Regatta and Carnival Committee and is in the shape of a square-rigged sail. The three-masted sailing ship in the centre, the lifeboat and the fish in the lower corners and the three cockle shells and oars below symbolise the town's connection with the sea, and the corn sheaf and plough in the upper corners its lesser link with agriculture.

Blakeney, a beautiful village and small harbour on the north Norfolk coast, possesses a fine sign which stands at one end of the quay. The ship in the centre records the three ships that were provided to Queen Elizabeth I to fight against the Spanish Armada. The fiddler and the cave-like hole on either side recall the story that a blind fiddler took a bet that he would fiddle his way down an underground passage, but he was never seen again. The waterfowl in the upper corners refer to the bird sanctuary at Blakeney Point. The hammers on the top of the sign are beetles used in clothmaking.

Langham is a small village a few miles inland from Blakeney. The sign, which stands opposite the Blue Bell, is a replacement of the original. On it, the ship commemorates the fact that Captain Marryat, the writer, once lived in the village and the turkey represents the turkey farm established on a wartime airfield nearby. Langham Hall was once the summer residence of the Bishop of Norwich — which accounts for the mitre surmounting the sign.

Holt. The sign, standing in front of Barclay's Bank, is two-sided. On one side is the figure of Sir John Gresham, former Lord Mayor of London, who in 1554 founded the free grammar school which later became Gresham's School. On the other side, in contrast, is Alice Perera, a notorious character of the fourteenth century. The owl on the top records that once a captured owl was put into the market pound. Even today the people of Holt are sometimes known as Holt Owls — this being also the name of the local football club.

Trunch. A little north of North Walsham is the village of Trunch. The church appears in the centre of the painted ironwork sign; at one side is the local brewery, built in 1837 but now closed, and at the other are a tractor and plough. The two smaller objects below are the village pump and the magnificent medieval font cover in the church. The sign is at the village crossroads, almost opposite the church.

Bodham, on the road from Holt to Cromer, gets its name, according to the Domesday Book, from a tax-collector named Boda who lived in the village. The sign, at the road junction in the village, shows him as a benevolent old man, apparently collecting taxes in kind.

Overstrand, on the coast just east of Cromer, possesses a two-sided sign on the Mundesley to Cromer road, at the corner of the High Street and the road to the beach, which records much of the village's past. The side shown in the photograph depicts a shipwreck, with one survivor who is being met by a local woman innkeeper, Rebecca Hythe, who was well known to sailors and smugglers. On the other side can be found the figures of a Dane and a Saxon, recording the struggles between these two peoples in the past, and a black dog, a fearsome legendary creature known as Black Shuck, who was said to bring misfortune if sighted. A crab and a poppy also appear on this interesting sign, the local crabs being amongst the finest and the poppy recalling the name Poppyland given to the area because of the countless poppies which grew there.

Swafield, a small village a little north of North Walsham, possesses an unusual and arresting sign. Made of metal and standing out against the sky is a wherry, such as used to carry coal from Great Yarmouth to Swafield Staithe. The massive post supporting the sign was the pivot of the post mill which once stood in the village. The sign is at the entrance to the village from North Walsham.

Paston, a small village a few miles south-east of Cromer on the coast road, is noteworthy as the home of the Paston family, writers of the famous Paston letters of the fifteenth century. Its most striking feature is the large Paston Barn, an Elizabethan building of flint and thatch. There is also a restored windmill. The unusual swinging sign, at the side of the road by the post office, records all these features.

Happisburgh, pronounced Haisborough, a village on the north-east coast of Norfolk south-east of Cromer, has strong connections with the sea, including a prominent lighthouse. Its church has a tower 110 feet (34 m) high, which has long served as a landmark for sailors, and in the churchyard lie more than a hundred sailors shipwrecked on the dangerous Happisburgh sands. The church also contains a beautiful octagonal font, at which it is recorded that on Whit Sunday 1793 the parson baptised 120 children. The sign, which stands by the road below the church, depicts the baptism at the font, the church and the lighthouse, together with a lifeboat and, representing the agricultural activity of the village, some corn. The figures on either side are Edric, a Danish overlord of the eleventh century, and Maud, a daughter of Roger Bigod, who received the manor from the king in about 1100 and was thought to have been buried here.

Worstead. The cloth called worsted, which is now produced in Yorkshire, was originally made in Worstead, south of North Walsham. Now just a charming village, in which a number of the old weavers' houses are still to be found, it was in the past a fair-sized town, with two churches; and its present church is one of the great ones of Norfolk. The sign, standing just outside the west end of the church, shows the church, with a horned sheep and the coat of arms of the Worstead family.

Felthorpe, a few miles north-west of Norwich, has an unusually shaped sign. It is a circular drum, on which is a painting of Felthorpe Hall, a fine residence noted for its numerous daffodils. The sign, which stands near the village hall, is made entirely of metal — appropriately, as the manufacture of agricultural implements was once a local industry.

Hevingham, between Norwich and Aylsham, is a village which was noted for its broom making. The village sign, which stands on the green in the part of the village known as Westgate, recalls this with its crossed brooms against a background which includes the church. The sign was the idea of one of the last of the brushmakers in the village.

South Walsham is near the broad named after it and not far from Acle. On the green stands the sign, which was given by the local Women's Institute. In Saxon times the people were in constant fear of invasion by the Vikings, and the sign shows a Viking ship sailing up the river, watched by a Saxon warrior. Behind are the two village churches, one now in ruins, and a wind pump.

Sprowston. The sign, wrought in metal and painted bright red, is outstanding. It is the work of Sprowston Secondary School and stands at the side of the road from Norwich to Wroxham. The post mill depicted on it appears in a number of pictures by John Crome, one of which is in the National Gallery. The mill was burnt down in 1933. A falcon is shown hovering above the fifteenth-century parish church, falconry having been practised here in the past.

Thorpe End is a pleasant garden suburb a few miles east of Norwich. The sign, which stands on a green by the side of the Norwich to Acle road, has the sky as its background. The central carving in wood of an oak tree in a triangular frame formed the original sign, the work of an architect who designed a number of the local houses. It was later enclosed in the wrought iron frame with the figures of a man and a woman gardening.

Salhouse is one of several attractive villages lying a few miles north-west of Norwich, in an area in which reeds are cut for Norfolk reed thatching, the best and longest lasting type of thatch. The name Salhouse is derived from sallow, a dwarf species of willow, out of which pegs are made for thatching. The sign, which is carved and brightly painted, stands on a triangle of grass before the Bell Inn. On it are shown two men cutting reeds, with a boat sailing on the nearby broad, and, above, an arch of sallows supporting the name of the village.

Potter Heigham has two village signs. One is in the old village and the other, illustrated here, is by the medieval bridge about a mile away. On one side are two Roman potters; pottery was produced in the old village in Roman times. On the other, the scene of sailing boats, a fisherman and a birdwatcher refers to present-day pastimes; and below is a man digging peat. Surmounting this colourful sign is the arched bridge.

Somerleyton is recorded in the Domesday Book as *Sumeledetun,* meaning a summer expedition or band of plundering Danes. The sign, which stands in the centre of the village, portrays a Viking and his ship and was erected in the village by Lord and Lady Somerleyton on the occasion of their silver wedding anniversary in 1949.

Beccles was once a flourishing port but now caters mainly for Broadland cruisers and yachts. Its handsome houses are mostly Georgian, as most of the Tudor buildings were destroyed by fires; but the sign tells of these earlier times for it shows Queen Elizabeth I presenting the municipal charter to the Port Reeve. It stands in a commanding position on the Bungay road.

Loddon is a delightful town of beautiful eighteenth-and early nineteenth-century buildings, and the houses built by the local council blend perfectly with these. The sign is a striking figure, cast in bronze, of Alfric, called Modercope, the original Saxon lord of Loddon, who gave the lordship to Bury St Edmunds Abbey in the reign of Edward the Confessor. His hand rests on a replica of the poor box, cut out of solid oak, which is in the church and said to be one of the oldest in England. The sign is at the crossroads, almost opposite the church.

Martham lies between the coast at Winterton and the Norfolk Broadland, and so the sign, which stands on the green, shows on one side a Saxon woman pleading for mercy from a Viking invader and on the other a Norfolk wherry, typical of those which traded on the rivers, and a windmill pump, such as was used to drain the marshes.

Caister-on-Sea, on the coast north of Yarmouth, was an important town in Roman times. Today it is notable for its fishing community and for its lifeboat, which has saved many lives on this dangerous coast. The carved wooden sign, which stands in the town in front of the police station, depicts on one side the head of a Roman soldier and on the other a lifeboat of early design battling against the seas.

Geldeston, a village north-west of Beccles, lies amidst beautiful countryside on the Norfolk-Suffolk border. Its carved and painted sign stands on the green and illustrates various features of the countryside and the many activities which used to be or still are carried on around. In the centre is a wherry, such as used to carry corn, seen sailing up the river to the old maltings.

Framingham Earl is south-east of Norwich near the Bungay road, and its sign, which is by the side of this road, stands out sharply as it is made of pierced and wrought iron and painted. The figure in the centre is the Earl of Norfolk — the Earl in the village name — and he is surrounded by tall trees, recording the trees planted in and around the village during the nineteenth century by an eminent Norwich surgeon, Edward Rigby, whose tombstone is in the churchyard of the Saxon-Norman church.

Earsham, just west of Bungay, is well known as the headquarters of the Otter Trust, whose lands include three lakes and a small stream, as well as breeding enclosures for the otters; it is a beautiful and peaceful place to visit. The sign, which is opposite the road to the hall, shows an otter surmounting a scene which includes the watermill, no longer in use, as it was in 1793.

Bungay is a town which has been an important crossing place of the river Waveney at least since Roman times, and its present castle was built by Roger Bigod in 1294 on the site of an even earlier one. The castle appears arrestingly on the sign, which stands at the entrance to the town on the Ipswich road.

Trowse Newton lies a few miles south-east of Norwich on the Beccles road, and the sign stands on the main road by the bridge. It illustrates the legend that a villager, disgruntled with his neighbours, built himself a house in a tree. The name Trowse is derived from the Old English *tre-hus*, tree house.

Saxlingham Nethergate, a village several miles south of Norwich, possesses many trees and a beautiful Elizabethan hall. On the green, before the church and the hall, stands the carved oak sign, which shows the figure of a Saxon who founded the village in AD 832.

Wymondham is a town with fine old buildings and an equally fine abbey, and its two-sided sign, which is at the corner of Church Street in front of the county library, tells of its past. On one side Robert Kett, a Wymondham man who became the leader of the rebellion against the enclosure of common lands, is seen encouraging others to join with him. On the other is a wood-turner, for Wymondham was noted for this work and the arms of the town, which appear below, bear a wooden spoon crossed by a spigot. Over all is a carved model of the abbey, before which stands a Benedictine monk.

Hempnall is a village on the B1135 road from Bungay to Wymondham. John Wesley came here to preach in 1754 and recorded in his journal: 'The ring leader of the mob came with his horn, as usual, before I began, but one quickly catched and threw away his horn, and in a few minutes he was deserted by all his companions who were seriously attentive to the great truth. By grace ye are saved through faith.' The occasion is shown on the village sign, which is a fine example of work produced by combined local effort and talent. It stands at the road junction near the church.

Hingham is a large village a few miles east of Watton. It was here that Samuel Lincoln, an ancestor of Abraham, worked as a weaver, before going to Norwich and finally to America in the steps of the Pilgrim Fathers. They and their ships are represented on the sign, which stands on the green by the post office.

Hethersett, a few miles from Wymondham on the way to Norwich, is skirted by the A11 road, and the sign stands just off this road at the Norwich end of the village. It is finely carved in natural wood and shows the fourteenth-century church, a deer, referring to the village's old name of *Hederseta,* meaning an enclosure for deer, and a formal-style oak tree representing the tree still standing by the side of the A11, under which Robert Kett is said to have raised his rebellion in 1549.

Fritton, east of Long Stratton, possesses a large common. This can be pleasantly viewed from the village sign, which is situated on a corner of the common and has a hexagonal base which provides seats all round. The figure of the ploughman shows that this is an agricultural area and the squirrel. and the owl on the brackets typify the wildlife.

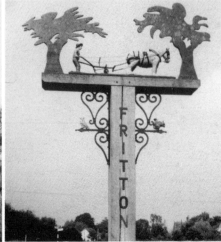

23

East Harling, some miles north-east of Thetford, has a finely carved sign with various motifs on the post and, above, an enchanting lamb symbolising the Lamb Fair which was held annually in July. Standing on the village green, it was presented by the Boy Scouts on the occasion of the coronation of Queen Elizabeth II in 1953.

Quidenham is a small village surrounded by woodland, lying off the Thetford to Norwich road. It is believed to be the burial place of Boadicea, or Boudica, the queen of the Iceni and she appears on the sign driving her chariot. The sign, of wrought iron and painted, is to be found on the village green, where it stands out clearly against the sky.

Bressingham, a village to the west of Diss, is known for its park-like plant nursery and collection of steam engines. These are on the road from Diss to Thetford, but the village and the church are a little to the north of it, and the sign, erected to commemorate the golden jubilee in 1973 of the local Women's Institute, is in the village at Pillar Box Corner. The original church was built in 1280 by Sir Richard Boyland, a judge who was fined 4000 marks by King Edward II for corruption. The sign portrays him, standing in front of the church.

Thetford, on the Norfolk-Suffolk border, is a town which is a mixture of old flint and timber-framed houses and new industrial buildings. The sign, which stands on the right of the A11 road from London, is two-sided. On one side stands Sweyne, king of the Danes, who made Thetford his capital and died there, and on the other Thomas Paine, author of *The Rights of Man* and supporter of the American Revolution, who was born there in 1737.

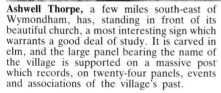

Ashwell Thorpe, a few miles south-east of Wymondham, has, standing in front of its beautiful church, a most interesting sign which warrants a good deal of study. It is carved in elm, and the large panel bearing the name of the village is supported on a massive post which records, on twenty-four panels, events and associations of the village's past.

Diss, on the river Waveney just inside the Nokfolk border, is a bustling modern town but has many old houses dating back to Tudor times. It is built round a 6 acre (2.4 ha) mere or lake, beside which stands the two-sided sign. John Skelton, rector of Diss from 1504 to 1529 and Poet Laureate, was tutor to the children of Henry VII and is shown, on one side of the sign, with the royal children. On the other side are two figures of an earlier period, explained on a plate below.

Southwold is a delightful town on the Suffolk coast which has a number of Georgian houses and a small musueum. The sign, which is across the road from the post office, depicts two men of war, one flying the British flag, the other the Dutch, commemorating the terrible and indecisive Battle of Sole Bay fought, in full view of the townsfolk, between the English and the Dutch fleets in 1672.

Kenninghall lies in the centre of the triangle formed by Thetford, Diss and Attleborough. On the green at the crossroads is the brightly coloured wrought iron sign. The coats of arms on the four shields are those of Edward the Confessor (top), the Howards, Dukes of Norfolk (left), the Earl of Mowbray (right) and the Earl of Albemarle (below). The riderless horse and the hound, the badge of the Talbots, both represent carvings in the village church. At the top of the sign is the Kenninghall Brooch, an Anglo-Saxon ornament found near where the sign stands.

Scole, which lies just in Norfolk on the border with Suffolk, has been a staging post of importance since Roman times, the name meaning a shelter. The sign stands on a green by the war memorial, not far from the White Hart, a posting inn built in 1655. On the sign is the head of a Roman eagle and crossed posthorns. Below are the shields of two families who were lords of the manor and the saltire of St Andrew, to whom the nearby church is dedicated.

Pulham St Mary, north-east of Scole, has an unusual motif for its sign, which stands in the centre of the village. The airship tethered to its mooring mast is the R33, sometimes known as the Pulham Pig, which was housed in a hangar near the former Pulham railway station

Fressingfield, a village midway between Scole and Halesworth, is noted for its inn, the Fox and Goose, and for one of the finest small churches in Suffolk. It was the site of a pilgrims' hospice, being on the route to the shrine at Walsingham from the port of Dunwich. This is recalled in the village sign showing a pilgrim with his mule.

26

Walberswick, a village of great charm on the Suffolk coast across the River Blyth from Southwold, was once a much bigger place. There are many large old houses, and ships were built and manned there. Its painted copper sign of a sailing ship (above left) stands commandingly on the grassy bank beside the road at the entrance to the village.

Westleton is a fine village a few miles inland from Dunwich on the Suffolk coast. The sign, which is of wrought iron painted black and white, depicts the old windmill which stood in the village until its demolition in 1963. A sail beam of the old mill forms the post for the sign and at the base is a millstone. The sign stands prominently at the top of the village green.

Middleton, down a turning off the A12 road at Yoxford, is a delightful and almost hidden Suffolk village. Its two-sided sign, showing on one side a colourful cock and on the other the church, before which it stands, is unique, being made of mosaic, the work of a local artist.

Kelsale cum Carlton has, standing on the A12 Ipswich to Yarmouth road, a wrought iron sign of the kind frequently found in villages in this area. Kelsale is noted for its vineyard and in the centre of the sign hangs a bunch of grapes and circling this are the eight bells of the church.

Sibton. Near Yoxford on the Yoxford to Stowmarket road is the village of Sibton, and on a high bank opposite the church is the village sign, standing out sharply against the sky. The monks in white habits and the sheep record that the Cistercian monastery in Sibton was the only one in Suffolk where the monks were sheep farmers.

Peasenhall is a few miles along the road from Sibton towards Stowmarket, and the sign is by this road in the centre of the village. Of wrought iron and painted, it is a model of a Smyth seed-drill, such as was made in the Peasenhall works of Smyth and Son from 1800 to 1967.

Haughley, a few miles north of Stowmarket, has, standing in the centre of the village, a wrought iron sign representing a motte and bailey castle, the remains of which are to be found at the northern end of the village.

Brandeston is a small village away from the main roads a few miles south-west of Framlingham. Its wrought iron sign is on a triangle of grass opposite the Queen's Head. On it, the hanging figure beside the fourteenth-century church is that of one of its past vicars, John Lowes, who was hanged for witchcraft in 1646; and the cottage is that reputedly used as a hideaway by the famous smuggler Margaret Catchpole, who was finally deported to New South Wales. The arms above are those of the Revetts, an old Brandeston family and benefactors of the church.

28

Woolpit, a most attractive village east of Bury St Edmunds, gets its name from having had pits for trapping wolves. Its beautiful church has a Victorian spire which can be seen for miles around. It also has a legend of two Green Children, a boy and a girl, who, in the reign of King Stephen, came out of the ground into a harvest field and were cared for in the village, gradually losing their green colour when their diet was changed from bean pith to bread; the girl eventually married a man from King's Lynn, but the boy died soon after baptism. A wolf, the church spire and the children appear on the wrought iron sign which stands beside the church — the children appropriately painted green.

Drinkstone is a few miles east of Bury St Edmunds, and its sign is to be found at Drinkstone Green, at the entrance to a close of new houses. Designed and carved by a local resident from an oak cut from a nearby estate, it depicts a mill which still stands outside Drinkstone and it is protected by a roof of wooden shingles.

Earl Soham lies midway between Stowmarket and Yoxford, and standing on the green, surrounded by fine trees, is a most striking sign. In medieval times Earl Soham was a centre for falconry, and the tall carved figure of a falconer with his bird recalls this sport. The Women's Institute commissioned the Ipswich School of Art to do the work and the sign was erected in 1953 to commemorate the Queen's coronation. It was restored in 1979.

West Stow, north of Bury St Edmunds, is the site of an Anglo-Saxon settlement, which the St Edmundsbury Borough Council has made into a country park, with pleasant woodland and walks, around a reconstruction of the settlement. Two of these Anglo-Saxon houses appear on the sign, which stands in the village at the junction of the Bury St Edmunds and Mildenhall roads and was painted by the art master of the nearby Culford School and erected in 1977 by the Women's Institute.

Stonham Parva is close to the A140 road from Ipswich to Norwich. Its painted wrought iron sign recalls that this road has long been an important highway, along which many coaches used to travel. The magpie represents the coaching inn of that name which still stands in the village. The sign, which is not easily found, is in the village on the main road.

Great Finborough, a pleasant village just south-west of Stowmarket, has a fine wrought iron sign standing on the green, not far from the tall-spired church. It is well sited and stands out clearly against the sky. The tall oak in the centre represents one of many planted by the squire, and the man and woman and sheaf of corn symbolise life and fertility. The border of chestnut leaves refers to the numerous chestnut trees in the locality.

Pakenham, north-east of Bury St Edmunds, has both a windmill and a watermill. They both appear, under a carving of the church, on the sign, which stands in the village beside the village hall.

Easton, a few miles north-west of Wickham Market, well warrants a visit for it is a charming setting of houses, large and small, surrounded by fine trees. It is also the home of the Easton Harriers, and this is the subject of the village sign, which stands on grass beside the road below the church. The background to the placename represents the crinkle-crankle wall of the Easton Park estate.

Orford, although an important port in Elizabethan times, is now only a large village. Its imposing castle was built by Henry II in 1165. The keep, which is all that remains, was the first in England to be built in hexagonal shape. Its dungeon, according to a fifteenth-century story, once held a Wild Man, half man and half fish, who was caught in a fisherman's net but later escaped back into the sea. The sign, which stands at the entrance to the village, by the school, depicts the castle.

Benhall. The wrought iron sign stands at the entrance to the village on the A12 Ipswich to Yarmouth road, just south of Saxmundham. The Suffolk plough, supported by half wheels, is painted blue. The sign was put up in memory of the village postmaster, Ted Ayden.

FURTHER READING

Proctor, Frances, and Miller, Philippa. *Village Signs in Norfolk.*
Proctor, Frances, and Miller, Philippa. *100 More Village Signs of the County of Norfolk.*
Proctor, Frances, and Miller, Philippa. *Book 3, Village Signs of Norfolk.*

INDEX

ACKNOWLEDGEMENTS

I gratefully acknowledge the help I have received from several people: Mrs Molly Carter, whose appreciation of and enthusiasm for her late husband's work, and the help she gave me, greatly contributed to this book; Philippa Miller and Frances Proctor, who allowed me to use their photographs of the signs of the villages on the Sandringham estate; Mr E. F. Hardy of Stowmarket, whose well illustrated talk on village signs initially inspired me to write this book and who gave me help later; and last, but by no means least, my husband, who has given me great encouragement and assistance.